Men-at-Arms • 71

The British Army 1965–80

D G Smith • Illustrated by Angus McBride

Series editor Martin Windrow

First published in Great Britain in 1977 by Osprey Publishing,
Midland House, West Way, Botley, Oxford OX2 0PH, UK
44-02 23rd St, Suite 219, Long Island City, NY 11101, USA
E-mail: info@ospreypublishing.com

Transferred to digital print on demand 2010

First published 1977
8th impression 2005

Printed and bound by PrintOnDemand-Worldwide.com, Peterborough, UK

A CIP catalogue record for this book is available from the British Library

ISBN: 978 0 85045 273 0

Series Editor: Martin Windrow
Filmset by BAS Printers, Over Wallop, Hampshire

Author's Note

This book represents, at best, a thumbnail sketch; ceremonial dress and No. 1 Dress (the old 'Blues') have been excluded. It should
be emphasized that the information given is that which was authorized in spring 1976. By publication date it is likely that some
details of badges, buttons, belts and headwear will have changed. For reasons of space certain supporting Corps have had to
be omitted altogether.

I would like to express my thanks to all my colleagues in the Ministry of Defence, in particular Maj Frank Croxford; to the many
regimental secretaries and other individuals who have helped in the supply and confirmation of uniform detail; and to Mrs R. Burdett
who slaved away over a typewriter for so long. My special thanks are due to the staff of Soldier magazine who have been most
helpful in the supply of illustrations.

FOR A CATALOGUE OF ALL BOOKS PUBLISHED BY OSPREY
MILITARY AND AVIATION PLEASE CONTACT:

Osprey Direct, c/o Random House Distribution Center,
400 Hahn Road, Westminster, MD 21157
Email: uscustomerservice@ospreypublishing.com

Osprey Direct, The Book Service Ltd, Distribution Centre,
Colchester Road, Frating Green, Colchester, Essex, CO7 7DW
E-mail: customerservice@ospreypublishing.com

www.ospreypublishing.com

Standard Items and Terms

Unless specifically stated otherwise, the following may be assumed for each corps listed:

Officer's SD: Infantry pattern, with Sam Browne belt. No. 2 Dress cap, khaki with brown chinstrap. Brown gloves and shoes. Light-khaki shirt and tie.

Soldiers' SD: English pattern. Medium-khaki shirt, dark-khaki tie, khaki wool gloves, black boots DMS or shoes. White waistbelt, rectangular brass buckle plate bearing regimental cap plate (for parade).

Buttons: All 'brass' (yellow anodized aluminium) except Royal Green Jackets, Royal Irish Rangers and Ghurka regiments (black).

Shoulder Titles: Only cavalry soldiers wear these in SD; officers and soldiers may wear them on shirtsleeve order or barrack jersey.

Jerseys: Standard pattern khaki, with round neck, worn in winter barrack, combat and fatigue dress; in summer the shirt is worn with sleeves rolled to 1 in. above elbows. 1975 dark-green barrack dress trousers are often seen, either with stable belt or dark-green 'courlene' working belt with matt black 1937-pattern fittings.

Ranking: Except for WOIs full-colour coats-of-arms, ranks, trade and skill-at-arms badges are white on khaki for all corps except those specified otherwise in text.

SD Jackets: Foot Guards officers—Dark khaki, no collar badges, plain patch top pockets with buttoned 3-point flaps, inset side pockets with 3-point flaps without buttons, two rear vents, plain cuffs; number of front and cuff buttons varying with the regiment. *Royal Armoured Corps officers—* Four front buttons, plain patch top pockets with buttoned single-point flaps, inset slanted side pockets with 'rectangular' flaps without buttons,

plain two-button cuffs, single rear vent. *Infantry pattern officers—* Four front buttons, box-pleated top pockets with buttoned 3-point flaps, 'bellows' side pockets with buttoned rectangular flaps, Polish cuffs without buttons, single rear vent. *Highland pattern officers—* As Infantry but cutaway rounded front bottom edges, the patch side pockets cut to follow this line; two rear vents.

Soldiers' SD Jackets: English pattern— Four front buttons, box-pleated top pockets with buttoned

Regimental Sergeant Major, Coldstream Guards, demonstrating one of the movements during the 'Salute'. The peak of the No. 1 Dress cap has the five rows of gold braid appropriate to this rank. The Guards WO's special large rank badge worn on the upper sleeve may be seen clearly here. The sash and white belt (here, the old buff leather type) are worn for parades. (MOD)

Private, Grenadier Guards, wearing the Service Dress which replaced the Battle Dress. The red and blue No. 1 Dress cap has a plain brass edging, indicating rank. This is a peculiarity of Foot Guards; so is the 'Trained Soldier' badge on the sleeve. On the shoulder strap may be seen the regimental title 'GG' below the crest. (MOD)

pattern are specifically mentioned in the body of the te* Lancer regiments have 'quarter welts' to their No. Dress caps, running vertically from the band to th crown welt at front, back, and each side. Scottis regiments do not wear No. 1 or No. 2 Dress cap having instead a Glengarry or bonnet of regiment. pattern, the badge worn on the left side; instea of the beret they wear a khaki bonnet with kha toorie and the badge on the left, usually backed b a piece of regimental tartan. Officers and men c services (e.g., RAMC, RAOC, REME, RAPC AAC) attached to an infantry or cavalry regimer will often wear some of the 'tribal items' of th

single-point flaps, inset side pockets with rectangular flap, plain cuff without buttons, single rear vent; longer skirts than either of the Scottish pattern jackets. *Highland pattern*—As English but three front buttons, front ends of skirts rounded off, two rear vents. *Lowland pattern*—As Highland with slightly longer skirts.

Caps: The 'Royal' pattern No. 1 Dress cap worn by many regiments and corps is dark blue with red band and red crown piping. *Only variations from this*

arent unit (e.g., Glengarry, lanyard, foreign
istinction, etc).

ervice Dress, General

n cavalry regiments the regimental cap badge is
ustomarily worn on a cloth backing on the upper
ight arm by corporals and above, and below the
varrant badge by WOs. Officers of cavalry and
rtillery usually wear a brown leather crossbelt and
ouch with whistle on the chest; officers of
ngineers, Royal Signals, infantry and supporting
ervices usually wear brown leather Sam Browne
vaistbelts with a supporting strap over the right
houlder.

Officers and soldiers may wear No. 1 Dress caps
with No. 2 Dress for parades. On other occasions
officers will wear either the khaki No. 2 Dress cap or
regimental sidehat while soldiers will wear either
the sidehat or the beret. Warrant Officers 1st Class
(WOIs) will wear officer-pattern hats, gloves, shoes
and embellishments.

OFFICERS' BADGES OF RANK

(worn on both shoulders in regimental pattern and
colour)

Second Lieutenant, Lieutenant, Captain : Respectively
one, two and three stars.
Major, Lieutenant Colonel : Respectively a crown, and
a crown over one star. Plain gold edging to peak of
No. 1 Dress cap.
Colonel : A crown over two stars. Brass buttons with
royal cypher within Garter. Gorget patches with
crimson lace and brass button. Embroidered lion
over crown cap badge, red cap band, gold
oakleaves on No. 1 Dress cap peak.
Brigadier : A crown over three stars in triangular
formation, otherwise as Colonel.
Major General : A star over crossed baton and sabre.
Buttons with crossed baton and sabre within
wreath. Gorget patches with gold oakleaf embroidery, small button (plain double gold piping in
Nos. 6, 8 and 9 Dress). Cap badge of lion and
crown, over crossed baton and sabre within wreath,
in gold. Gold oakleaf edging top and bottom of cap
peak.
Lieutenant General : A crown over crossed baton and
sabre, otherwise as Major General.
General : A crown over a star over crossed baton and

Staff Sergeant, RASC, wearing red-over-blue shoulder patch
with white bayonet, identifying the School of Infantry. He
wears the old Battle Dress which served the Army well, in
various forms, from the late 1930s to the 1960s. The Mk 4
helmet is worn, with '37-pattern webbing—here, 'skeleton
order'. 'Boots General Service', which made the traditional
satisfying crunch on the parade square, are now issued only to
the Guards and a few other units; other soldiers wear 'Boots,
Direct Moulded Sole'. The crossed rifles above the crown and
chevrons of rank denote a marksman. (MOD)

sabre, otherwise as Lieutenant General.
Field Marshal : A crown over crossed batons within
wreath. Buttons with crossed batons within wreath.
Cap badge of lion and crown, over crossed batons
within wreath, in gold. Otherwise as for General.
(*Gorget Patches* for Colonel and above are scarlet

5

Infantryman in full DPM combat clothing and '58-pattern webbing, with the GPMG tripod-mounted in its sustained fire role.

except for following corps: RAMC—dull cherry; RAChD—purple; RAPC—primrose; RAVC—maroon; RAEC—Cambridge blue; RADC—emerald green; ACC—grebe grey; WRAC—beech brown.)

NCOs' AND WARRANT OFFICERS' BADGES OF RANK

(All chevrons point downwards unless otherwise stated. Key: Foot Guards=FG, Household Cavalry=HC)

Conductor RAOC: Royal Arms within blue laurels, within red ring, on lower sleeve.
WOI: Royal Arms, with regimental surround if worn.

RSM, RCM (HC), Superintending Clerks (FG): As above without surround; on upper sleeve by RSMs (FG).
WOII: Crown within wreath on lower sleeve for RQMS, RQMC (HC), Orderly Room QMS (FG), Farrier QMC (HC). Crown alone for CSM, SSM, BSM, and SCM (HC).
NCOs:
SQMC and Staff Corporal (HC): Crown above 4-bar chevrons, point up, both forearms.
Colour Sgt, CQMS, Staff Sgt; Corporal of Horse and Band Corporal of Horse (HC): Crown above 3-bar chevrons, both upper arms.
Trumpet Major: Crossed trumpets above 4-bar chevrons, point up, on both forearms. In HC, a crown above the trumpets. *Drum Majors* as Trumpet Majors but with drum replacing crossed trumpets. *Bugle Majors* as above but bugle replacing drum. *Pipe Majors* as above but bagpipes

eplacing drum. *Pipe Major (FG)*, 4-bar chevrons, point up.

Sergeant: 3-bar chevrons, both upper arms.

Corporal and Lance Corporal (HC): Crown above 2-bar chevrons, as above.

Corporal, Bombadier (RA): 2-bar chevrons, as above.

Lance Corporal, Lance Bombardier: 1-bar chevron, as above.

Key to listing of corps and regimental distinctions

(Note: Cap badges generally not described as they are illustrated on pp. 8, 9.)

DC: No. 1 Dress cap if different from Royal pattern

SH: Sidehat, if any

Bt: Beret

OSD: Officers' Service Dress. Jacket usually only described if different from normal design for corps or arm of service.

SSD: Soldiers' Service Dress. Jacket described only if different from English pattern.

B: Buttons

SB: Stable belt, if any.

CB: Collar badges, if any.

ST: Shoulder titles, if any.

J: Jersey, if not standard khaki.

C: Cravat, if any.

L: Lanyard, if any; worn on left shoulder unless otherwise specified.

Note: Omission of any heading indicates that relevant unit does not wear the item, with exception of No. 1 Dress cap.

The Household Division

HOUSEHOLD CAVALRY

The Life Guards

SH: Blue band and tip, scarlet top, no peak or buttons, all piped yellow. *Bt:* Blue. *OSD:* No. 2 Dress cap, gilt badge. Dark khaki, 4 front buttons, 2 cuff buttons, single vent, buttoned flaps to pleated top pockets and patch side pockets, plain cuff. *B:* Lion and crown over entwined reversed script

'LG'. Buff breeches, brown riding boots with buckled spurs, or trousers with turnups. *L:* Red, right shoulder. *SSD:* Standard khaki. *ST:* Brass 'LG'. White belt with brass plate bearing Royal Arms. *SB:* 3 equal stripes scarlet-blue-scarlet, brown leather buckles left side. *J:* Black polo-neck sometimes worn under olive-green coveralls.

The Blues and Royals

SH, Bt: As Life Guards. *OSD:* No. 2 Dress cap, dark bronze badge as Life Guards. *B:* Crown over

Sergeant of the Small Arms School Corps in jersey, stable belt, DPM trousers and '37 pattern web anklets demonstrates the Swingfire anti-tank missile launcher. The SASC wear a blue beret, silver cap badge, collar badges and buttons, and brass shoulder titles. The stable belt is dark green with narrow stripes of yellow, Oxford-blue and red, and silver '37-pattern fittings. (**MOD**)

British Army Cap Badges (Soldiers' patterns only): *Top row, l. to r.:* **(1) Life Guards (2) Blues and Royals (3) Royal Horse Artillery (4) Queen's Dragoon Guards (5) Royal Scots Dragoon Guards (6) 4th/7th Dragoon Guards (7) 5th Royal Inniskilling Dragoon guards (8) Queen's Own Hussars.** *Second row:* **(1) Royal Tank Regiment (2) Royal Artillery (3) Royal Engineers (4) Royal Signals (5) Grenadier Guards (6) Coldstream Guards (7) Scots Guards (8) Irish Guards.** *Third row:* **(1) Light Infantry (2) Prince of Wales's Own Regiment of Yorkshire (3) Green Howards (4) Royal Highland Fusiliers (5) Cheshire Regiment (6) Royal Welch Fusiliers (7) Royal Regiment of Wales (8) King's Own Scottish Borderers.** *Fourth row:* **(1) Black Watch (2) Duke of Edinburgh's Royal Regiment (3) Queen's Own Highlanders (4) Gordon Highlanders (5) Argyll & Sutherland Highlanders (6) Parachute Regiment.** *Bottom row:* **(1) Royal Electrical & Mechanical Engineers (2) Royal Military Police (3) Royal Army Pay Corps (4) Royal Army Veterinary Corps (5) Royal Military Academy Sandhurst Staff Band (6) Small Arms School Corps (7) Military Provost Staff Corps (8) Royal Army Education Corps. (COI)**

'RHG', over '1st D', both script. *L:* Blue, left shoulder. Upper left arm, Napoleonic eagle badge (see SSD) on black cloth backing. *SSD:* As Life Guards except *ST:* Brass 'BLUES & ROYALS'. Above these, facing front, brass Napoleonic eagle on plinth numbers '105'. *L:* White, left shoulder. *B:* As above. Black backing to metal rank badges. *SB:* As Life Guards but blue-scarlet-blue, buckle worn centrally. White belt as Life Guards. *J:* As Life Guards.

Royal Horse Artillery

See under Royal Artillery.

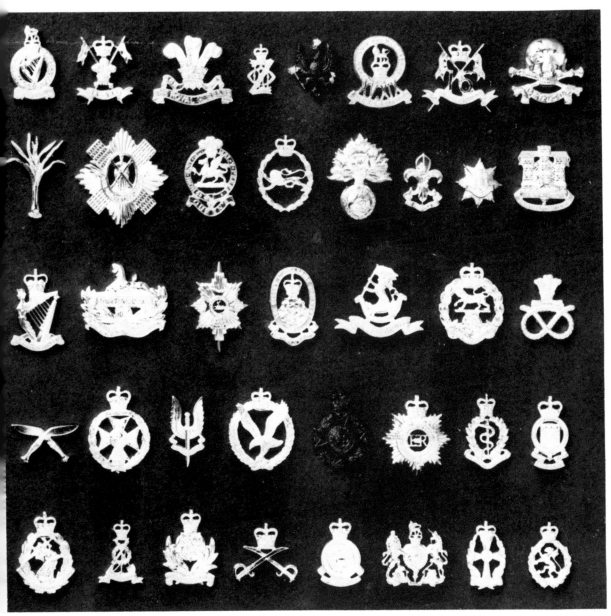

THE FOOT GUARDS

Grenadier Guards

DC: Royal, peak edging according to rank. *Bt:* Khaki. *OSD:* FG pattern, 3 front buttons, 2 cuff buttons. Cap and beret badge, gold wire flaming grenade on black backing. *B:* Gilt, a crown over entwined, reversed 'ER' over flaming grenade. *SSD: ST:* Crowned Garter containing entwined, reversed 'ER', above 'GG', all brass. *SB:* Equal stripes blue-red-blue, brown buckles front centre. Cap badges: WOs—flaming grenade in brass with

British Army Cap Badges (Soldiers' patterns only): *Top row, l. to r.:* (1) Queen's Royal Irish Hussars (2) 9th/12th Royal Lancers (3) Royal Hussars (4) 13th/18th Royal Hussars (5) 14th/20th King's Hussars (6) 15th/19th King's Royal Hussars (7) 16th/5th Queen's Royal Lancers (8) 17th/21st Lancers. *Second row:* (1) Welsh Guards (2) Royal Scots (3) Queen's Regiment (4) King's Own Royal Border Regiment (5) Royal Regiment of Fusiliers (6) King's Regiment (7) Royal Anglian Regiment (8) Devonshire & Dorset Regiment. *Third row:* (1) Royal Irish Rangers (2) Gloucestershire Regiment (3) Worcestershire & Sherwood Foresters Regiment (4) Queen's Lancashire Regiment (5) Duke of Wellington's Regiment (6) Royal Hampshire Regiment (7) Staffordshire Regiment. *Fourth row:* (1) Staff Band, Brigade of Gurkhas (2) Royal Green Jackets (3) Special Air Service Regiment (TA) (4) Army Air Corps (5) Royal Army Chaplains Department (6) Royal Corps of Transport (7) Royal Army Medical Corps (8) Royal Army Ordnance Corps. *Bottom row:* (1) Royal Army Dental Corps (2) Royal Pioneer Corps (3) Intelligence Corps (4) Army Physical Training Corps (5) Army Catering Corps (6) General Service Corps (7) Queen Alexandra's Royal Army Nursing Corps (8) Women's Royal Army Corps. (COI)

AAC Air Gunner at missile sights of helicopter. (*Soldier Magazine*)

crowned, entwined, reversed, 'ER' in silver; Sgts, bandsmen—as WOs but all brass; remainder—brass flaming grenade. *B:* As officers. White belt, brass plate bearing Royal Arms.

Coldstream Guards

DC: Blue, white band and piping, peak edging according to rank. *Bt:* Khaki. *OSD:* FG pattern, 3 groups each of 2 front buttons, 2 pairs of buttons each cuff. Cap and beret badge, silver Garter star, red cross, blue scrolls in oval form. *B:* Gilt Garter star in circular form. *SSD: ST:* Rose over 'CG', brass. Cap badges: Staff, Garter star, circular form, colours as officers; remainder, Garter star, circular, brass. *SB:* As Grenadier Guards. *B:* As officers. White belt as Grenadiers.

Scots Guards

DC: Blue, with scarlet, white and blue diced band, scarlet piping, peak edging according to rank. *Bt:* Khaki. *OSD:* FG pattern, 2 groups each of 3 front buttons, 3 buttons each cuff. Khaki No. 2 Dress cap

has small patch miniaturized Royal Stewart tart above each chinstrap button; rectangular pat behind beret badge. Cap and beret badge, silv star, gold thistle and band 'NEMO ME IMPUN LACESSIT' on blue centre. *B:* Gilt, crowned st of Order of Thistle. *SSD: ST:* Silver thistle abo brass 'SG'. *B:* As officers, but silver for pipers. Ca badges: Staff, Sgts, Musicians as officers but Stabrite; remainder, brass. White belt as Grenadi Guards. *SB:* As Grenadiers. *Pipers:* Highland S jackets; Royal Stewart tartan kilts; white Highlan purse with three black tassels on black belt; red an green marl stockings with plain red and gree dicing. Bagpipe covers are Black Watch tartar cords and ribbons are Royal Stewart.

Irish Guards

DC: Blue, green band and piping, peak edgin according to rank. *Bt:* Khaki. *OSD:* FG pattern, groups each of 4 front buttons, 4 buttons each cuf Cap and beret badge, star of Order of St Patrick i silver, white centre, red cross, green shamroc bearing three gold crowns, light-blue band bearin gold 'QUIS SEPARABIT MDCCLXXXIII'. *B* Gilt, crowned Irish harp facing left. *SSD: ST:* 'IG beneath cap badge. Cap badges: Staff, as officers remainder, same in Stabrite. *B:* As officers, bu silver for pipers. White belt and SB as Grenadiers *Pipers:* Highland SD jackets, saffron serge kilts Bagpipe covers, cords and ribbons olive-green.

Welsh Guards

DC: Blue, black band, peak edging according tc rank. *Bt:* Khaki. *OSD:* FG pattern, 5 front buttons, 5 buttons each cuff. *B:* Gilt, a leek below a crown; around it on a scroll 'CYMRU. AM. BYTH'. *SSD: ST:* Brass, 'WG' below the leek. *B:* As officers. White belt and SB as Grenadiers.

The Royal Armoured Corps

1st The Queen's Dragoon Guards

DC: Blue, white, band and piping. *SH:* Blue flaps, peak and tip, white body piped yellow, 2 yellow buttons. *Bt:* Blue. *OSD:* RAC pattern but 3 uttons each cuff. *CB:* Bronze, Gothic 'BAYS' within crowned bay-leaf wreath. *B:* 8-point star with crown covering top point; within this the Garter, within this 'Q' over 'DG', Gothic. Sam Browne with whistle on crossbelt. *SSD: ST:* Brass Gothic 'QDG'. *CB:* Silver 'BAYS'. Staff sgt's crowns are brass on blue backing. *L:* White, right shoulder. Brass 'BAYS' badge in crowned wreath on blue backing, upper left arm. White belt, silver rectangular plate. *B:* As officers. *SB:* Royal blue, leather buckles.

The Royal Scots Dragoon Guards (Carbiniers and Greys)

DC: Blue, blue piping, yellow vandyked band. *SH:* Blue, no peak or buttons, top of band piped yellow, yellow vandyking round band. *Bt:* Blue or light grey. *OSD:* Cap buttons bear silver thistle. On upper left arm, silver 'Prince of Wales' feathers badge, buttons brown leather, and the regimental title scroll. *CB:* As cap badge but on blue cloth patches. Turnups on trousers. *B:* Brass, showing regimental cap badge. *SSD:* *CB* and regimental arm badge as officers, also *B*, but cap buttons as jacket buttons. White belt, brass rectangular plate with cap badge. *Pipers:* Highland SD Jackets, brass buttons, Royal Stewart tartan kilts, 'Highland Purse No. 14' with badge and three black and scarlet tassels on black belt; stockings are red and green marl with plain red and green dicing. Bagpipe covers, cords and ribbons are Royal Stewart tartan.

4th/7th Royal Dragoon Guards

DC: Blue, Royal blue band and piping. *SH:* Blue flaps and tip piped yellow; red top, no peak or buttons. *Bt:* Blue, star-shaped red patch behind badge. *OSD:* *CB:* Small silver version of cap badge. *B:* Princess Mary's coronet over 'IV–VII'. Brown crossbelt with silver whistle and brass fittings. *SSD:* Badges and buttons as officers. *L:* White, right shoulder. *ST:* '4/7RDG', brass. Brown plastic belt with rectangular brass plate bearing cap badge. Regimental arm patch 1 in. below left shoulder, black diamond bearing one gold over two maroon chevrons. *SB:* Dark-red over narrow yellow central over dark-blue stripes. *C:* Black.

Sergeant, 1st Welsh Guards, in the Radfan area of southern Arabia in 1965. He wears the obsolete Khaki Drill uniform of shirt and shorts, with suede desert boots. (*Soldier Magazine*)

5th Royal Inniskilling Dragoon Guards

DC: Dark-green, primrose band and piping, dark-green backing to badges. *SH:* Dark-green flaps and peak piped primrose, primrose body and tip, 2 yellow buttons. *Bt:* Blue, dark-green shamrock-shaped patch behind badge. *OSD:* RAC but 3 buttons each cuff. Dark-green trousers. *CB:* Silver castles, flags flying inwards, above brass scroll with 'INNISKILLING'. *B:* Brass, with castle, flag to right, under 'V' and flanked by 'D' and 'G', within the motto 'VESTIGIA NULLA RETRORSUM'. Brown leather crossbelt; black shoes. *SSD:* *ST:* Brass '5DG' below Inniskilling castle badge without scroll, flags forward. *CB, B:* As officers. *L:* White, left shoulder. Dark-green trousers. White belt with brass '37-pattern fittings. Senior NCOs wear silver horse of Hanover on a dark-green patch on the right sleeve. *SB:* Red over narrow green central over yellow stripes, round silver buckle plate with Inniskilling castle over 'VDG'.

The Queen's Own Hussars

DC: Scarlet, scarlet band and piping. *SH:* Scarlet flaps, body and tip piped yellow, scarlet peak, 2

Definitive rear view of '58-pattern equipment, worn here without large pack. Clearly visible are the Mk 4 helmet, the Mk 1 haircut (!), the obsolete olive green temperate combat dress of the 1960s, the entrenching shovel (a new folding pattern is being procured), the Self-Loading Rifle, the short puttees which replaced the old web anklets, and the boots DMS. (*Soldier Magazine*)

The Queen's Royal Irish Hussars

DC: Scarlet, scarlet band and piping. *SH*: Office wear dark-green 'tent hat' with gold braid ar piping, shaped like stiffened version of Frenc Napoleonic stable cap; soldiers wear convention SH, green with yellow piping. *Bt*: Blue, gree headband. *OSD*: Buttons plain brass ball type. *CI* As cap badge, harps and lions facing inwards. Clot rank badges. Brown bandolier, brass picker equip ment, silver pouch with brass badge of entwine 'QRIH' under lion and crown. Same badge wor on officers' berets. *SSD*: *ST*: Brass 'QRIH'. *CB, B* As officers. *L*: Yellow, right shoulder. Corpora and above wear harp badge above chevrons; lanc corporals wear two chevrons. Green '37-patter waistbelt with rectangular brass plate bearin silver harp. *SB*: Green above narrow yellow abov narrow blue above green stripes. *J*: Green, V-nec for all ranks; soldiers wear brass 'QRIH' ST. *C* Dark-green.

9th/12th Royal Lancers (Prince of Wales's)

DC: Scarlet, scarlet band, blue piping anc quarter-welts. *SH*: Officers, dark-blue piped gold gold buttons; soldiers, red with yellow peak, pipinç and buttons. *Bt*: Blue. *OSD*: Box-pleated three point top pockets. *CB*: Smaller version of cap badge. *B*: Brass, crown above crossed lance behind entwined, reversed 'PW'. Sam Browne belt brass fittings. *SSD*: Brass CB as officers. *ST*: Brass 'IX/XIIL'. *L*: Red and yellow, left shoulder White waistbelt, rectangular silver plate bearing cap badge. *SB*: Yellow with narrow red edges, wider red central stripe; brown buckles, left. *C*: Red (khaki with combat dress).

The Royal Hussars (Prince of Wales's Own)

DC: Crimson, crimson band and piping. *SH*: Crimson, yellow piping and buttons. *Bt*: Reddish brown, oval-topped crimson patch behind badge. *OSD*: Khaki whipcord RAC jacket. Crimson trousers. Sam Browne with silver whistle on cross strap; black shoes. *B*: Flat brass, Prince of Wales's plume and motto; cap buttons domed, device in silver. *SSD*: Crimson trousers. *ST*: 'ROYAL' over 'HUSSARS', brass. *B*: As officers but cap buttons brass. *SB*: Equal yellow-red-yellow, the yellow stripes being edged at top and bottom of belt with dark blue. *J*: Officers, dark-green, with crimson

buttons. *Bt*: Blue. *OSD*: Plain patch top pockets with rectangular flaps, plain domed yellow buttons, inset side pockets with rectangular buttoned flaps, two rear vents. Brown leather crossbelt. 'Maid of Warsaw' badge on lower left arm. *CB*: Beneath a gold crown, interlaced, reversed silver 'QO', above blue and gilt scroll bearing 'THE QUEEN'S OWN HUSSARS'. *SSD*: *ST*: Brass 'QOH'. *CB*: Silver cypher, brass crown and scroll all on red path. *B*: Brass, plain domed. 'Maid of Warsaw' on lower left arm. White belt. *SB*: Equal stripes blue-yellow-blue, each with narrow central scarlet line; leather buckles on left. *J*: Officers wear lovat green, V-neck, white 'QOH' on khaki epaulettes. *C*: Blue.

paulettes bearing rank badges and shoulder titles
a brass.

3th/18th Royal Hussars (Queen Mary's Own)

DC: White, blue band, white piping. *SH:* Blue
flaps and peak, white body and tip, yellow buttons,
yellow piping to body and flaps. *Bt:* Blue. *OSD:*
CB: As cap badge, not facing inwards, gilt.
Trousers with turnups. *B:* Plain domed brass.
Brown bandolier with whistle. *SSD: ST:* Brass
'13/18H'. *CB:* Brass, as officers. Single cuff button.
L: White, right shoulder. Junior NCOs wear silver,
entwined 'QMO' on chevrons, senior NCOs and
WOs wear same in brass on chevrons or below
warrant badge. All soldiers wear diamond patch,
vertically halved white/dark-blue, on upper left
arm. White belt, rectangular brass plate with cap
badge. *SB:* Narrow dark-blue, wide white, wide
dark-blue, narrow white, wide dark-blue; brown
buckles, front centre. *J:* Officers, dark-green V-
neck.

14th/20th King's Hussars

DC: Scarlet, scarlet band and piping. *SH:* Scarlet,
yellow piping to body and flaps. *Bt:* Blue. Officers
wear gold eagle badge, senior NCOs the black
metal badge on lemon oval patch; tank crewmen
wear diagonally divided blue-over-yellow square
patch behind badge. *OSD: CB:* Lion and crown
within Garter above scroll with '14th/20th
HUSSARS'. Sam Browne with whistle on strap. *B:*
Flat brass, crown over 'XIV' over 'XX'. *SSD: ST:*
brass '14/20H'. *CB, B:* As Officers. All soldiers,
small silver crossed-kukris badge below each
shoulder. *SB:* Equal blue-lemon yellow-blue,
brown buckles, front centre. *J:* Officers, dark-
green, khaki epaulettes.

15th/19th The King's Royal Hussars

DC: Scarlet, scarlet band and piping. *SH:* Scarlet
flaps and body piped yellow, scarlet peak and tip,
two yellow buttons. *Bt:* Blue, red patch behind
badge. *OSD:* Rectangular buttoned flaps, all four
pockets. *CB:* Brass, lion over crown over scroll with
'MEREBIMUR'. Sam Browne, whistle on cross
strap. *B:* Lion over crown within Garter, above
scroll with 'THE KING'S-ROYAL-HUSSARS'.
Lion and crown only on cap buttons. *SSD: CB:* As

The light khaki 'pixie' suit, introduced in 1944 for tank crews, is
still to be seen in service. This motorcyclist with an RCT Tank
Transporter Unit wears it; note two zips from ankle to neck,
numerous pockets, and deep collar showing blanket material
lining. (MOD)

officers but smaller. *ST:* '15/19H', brass. NCOs,
WOs wear silver woven crown and lion badge on
right arm. White belt, silver plate, brass badge. *SB:*
Blue with twin centre stripe, yellow over red;
brown buckles, left. *C:* Blue.

16th/5th The Queen's Royal Lancers

DC: Scarlet, blue bands, piping and quarter welts.
SH: Blue flaps and red body piped yellow, blue
peak, white tip, two yellow buttons. *Bt:* Blue.
OSD: Box-pleated top pockets, lower pockets have
rectangular buttoned flap. Sam Browne with cross
strap worn back to front. *CB:* Silver; under crown
and on crossed lances, left, 'C' cypher within

British troops in Cyprus, displaying a large range of cap badges. *Top row, l. to r.:* **King's Own Royal Border Regiment, RAPC, AAC, RAOC, RMP in obsolete combat cap, RAPC, RCT, 4th/7th RDG, RPC.** *Second row:* **Royal Signals, REME, QDG, 13th/18th Royal Hussars, 17th/21st Lancers, RA, Intelligence Corps, Duke of Wellington's Regiment, RAMC, Royal Anglians.** *Front row:* **Intelligence Corps, Royal Hussars, RAOC, REME, Royal Irish Rangers, 2nd RTR. Note that many of these soldiers are on attachment to the Army Air Corps and wear their 'parent' cap badges on that Corps' light blue beret.** *(Soldier Magazine)*

Garter; right, crowned Irish harp within scroll with 'QUIS SEPARABIT'; below, scroll with 'THE QUEEN'S-ROYAL-LANCERS' *B:* On crossed lances, Irish harp within ring with 'FIFTH ROYAL IRISH' under crown, over shamrock sprigs. Cap buttons with crown, over 'QL' over '16'. *SSD: CB, B:* As officers, but cap buttons as tunic buttons. *ST:* Brass, '16/5L'. *SB:* Equal stripes, red over yellow over blue, brown buckles, left. *C:* Combat and barrack dress: A Sqn, red; B Sqn, blue; C Sqn, yellow; HQ, green.

17th/21st Lancers

DC: Blue, white band, piping and quarter welts. *SH:* Blue flaps and white body piped yellow, blue peak, white tip, two yellow buttons. *Bt:* Blue. *OSD:* As 16th/5th; Sam Browne. *CB:* Gilt skull, crossbones and scroll with 'OR GLORY'. *B:* Brass, with skull and crossbones. *SSD: CB:* As officers, silver. NCOs wear cap badge on right arm. White belt, silver plate with cap badge. *ST:* Brass, '17/21L'. *SB:* Dark blue, twin central narrow white stripes, silver plate as white belt.

Royal Tank Regiment (1st, 2nd, 3rd and 4th Regiments)

Ceremonial Bt: Black, wide black headband; for officers, two gold stripes around headband; silver badge, short brown-red-green cut feather hackle. *Working Bt:* Black. *OSD: CB:* Dark bronze, as cap badge. *B:* Crown over entwined 'RTR'. Black Sam Browne, black gloves and shoes, Ashplant walking stick. *SSD:* Silver CB as officers; black belt, silver plate and badge. *ST:* Brass, 'RTR'. All ranks except 1st RTR wear shoulder strap flashes: 2nd RTR, yellow with central brown, red, green stripe;

rd RTR, green; 4th RTR, blue. *L:* 1st, red; 2nd, ellow; 3rd, green; 4th, blue; depot, black. All anks and regiments, white tank badge upper right rm. *SB:* Equal stripes, green over red over brown; lack buckles, left. *J:* Officers and senior NCOs, lack, with regimental flashes on black epaulettes. oldiers, standard khaki. *C:* Red, yellow, green, lue for 1st, 2nd, 3rd, 4th respectively.

* * *

Royal Regiment of Artillery

H: Blue, red peak, body and tip, two yellow uttons. *Bt:* Blue; officers have gold wire cannon adge. *OSD:* RAC pattern. *CB:* Dark bronze laming grenade, scroll with 'UBIQUE'. *B:* Crown ver cannon. *SSD: CB:* As officers but smaller. White belt, silver plate with cap badge. *L:* White, eft shoulder. Senior NCOs wear white cannon adge above chevrons. *SB:* Red, blue central band with yellow central strip; brown buckles, left. *J:* Officers, dark-blue, dark-blue cloth epaulettes with brass buttons and ST 'RA'.

Royal Horse Artillery

As RA except: Soldiers' *CB:* 'EIIR' within crowned oval Garter above scroll with 'ROYAL HORSE ARTILLERY', all silver. *ST:* Brass, 'RHA'. Officers' beret badge, as CB in gold and blue wire on red backing. *SB:* Light blue, narrow yellow centre stripe; brown buckles, left.

Corps of Royal Engineers

DC: Blue, blue band, scarlet piping. *SH:* Blue, red piping to body and flaps, embroidered grenade badge. *Bt:* Blue; officers wear embroidered gold wire grenade badge. *OSD:* Infantry pattern. *CB:* As RA, no scroll. *B:* 'EIIR' under crown within Garter, on lower periphery 'ROYAL ENGINEERS'. *SSD: CB:* Brass, as officers but smaller. White belt, brass plate with cap badge. *L:* Blue, right shoulder, all ranks. *SB:* Red, two narrow blue stripes, round silver plate bearing cap badge. *C:* Blue.

Royal Corps of Signals

DC: Blue, blue band. *SH:* Blue flaps and peak, light blue body. *Bt:* Blue. *OSD:* Infantry pattern. *CB:* Mercury. Sam Browne. *SSD: CB:* As officers. *B:* All ranks, brass, with figure of Mercury. Black belt, brass plate with cap badge. *L:* Blue, right shoulder, all ranks. *SB:* Light-blue over dark-green

Two of the dozens of typical 'tribal items' added to regimental uniform over the years in memory of bygone battles and shared campaigns. Left, the silver-on-red 'Maid of Warsaw' badge worn on the left forearm by all ranks of the Queen's Own Hussars, in memory of service with 2nd Polish Corps in Italy in the Second World War. Right, the black diamond bearing one gold above two maroon chevrons worn high on the left arm by soldiers of the 4th/7th Royal Dragoon Guards.

with narrow dark-blue centre stripe; black buckles, left. *J:* Officers, dark-blue, dark-blue cloth epaulettes with brass buttons and ranking; soldiers, dark-blue or standard khaki.

The Scottish Division

The Royal Scots (The Royal Regiment); 1st Foot

Facings: Blue. *Glengarry:* Blue; scarlet, green and white dicing, scarlet toorie. *OSD:* Highland pattern. Cap badge as Scots Guards. *CB:* As cap badge, smaller, matt bronze. *B:* Bronze; St Andrew with cross on star, above 'THE ROYAL SCOTS'. Black Highland shoes. Trews, No. 8 Hunting Stewart tartan. *SSD, Bandsmen's, Drummers':* Lowland pattern. Trews, No. 8 tartan. Short plaid. *Cap badge* on red oval patch: pierced brass, St Andrew with his cross above scroll with 'THE ROYAL SCOTS', all on silver St Andrew's cross and 4-point star. *CB:* Brass, thistles leaning outwards over scroll with 'ROYAL SCOTS'. *ST:* Silver, 'RS'. *SB:* Strip of tartan; black buckles, left. *Pipers:* Royal Stewart tartan trews and kilt. Sporran badge; silver, St Andrew with cross within thistle wreath over scroll with 'THE ROYAL SCOTS'. White hair purse, two black tassels, on black belt, worn with kilt. Silver CB and buttons. Red and black marl footless stockings, plain red and black dicing. Highland pattern SD. Bagpipe cords, cover and ribbons, Royal Stewart tartan.

Royal Irish Rangers demonstrate the SMG to a group of soldiers. The regiment's distinctive bonnet is worn with Temperate DPM combat dress and '58-pattern webbing; note that the bayonet frog has been incorporated into the outer face of the left front pouch. Among the audience can be seen examples of the khaki bonnet worn in combat dress by Scottish regiments. (*Soldier* Magazine)

The Royal Highland Fusiliers (Princess Margaret's Own Glasgow and Ayrshire Regiment); 21st, 71st and 74th Foot

Facings: Blue. *Glengarry:* Blue; scarlet, green and white dicing, scarlet toorie. *OSD:* Highland pattern. *CB:* As cap badge but smaller, matt bronze. *B:* Brass, flaming grenade—wider spread flames than cap badge. Trews, No. 5A Mackenzie tartan (HLI sett). White spats, black brogue shoes. *SSD, Bandsmens', Drummers':* Lowland pattern. *CB:* As cap badge but smaller. *ST:* Brass, 'RHF'. *B:* As officers. Trews, No. 5A tartan. *Pipers:* Highland SD. No. 5A trews or Erskine tartan kilt. Bagpipe cords cover and ribbons, Erskine tartan. Footless green and red marl stockings, red and green dicing

overstriped red and green on opposite colours. White hair purse, three long black tassels, silver badge of St Andrew with his cross on sprig of thistles; black belt.

The King's Own Scottish Borderers; 25th Foot

Facings: Blue. *Glengarry:* Blue; scarlet, green and white dicing, scarlet toorie. *OSD:* Highland pattern. *CB:* Dark bronze, three-towered castle on thistles over scroll with 'THE KING'S OWN/ SCOTTISH/ BORDERERS'. *B:* Brass, lion over crown, peripheral inscription 'KING'S OWN SCOTTISH BORDERERS'. Trews, No. 7 Leslie tartan. Black Highland shoes. *SSD, Bandsmens', Drummers':* Lowland pattern. *B:* As officers. *CB:* Brass, otherwise as officers. *ST:* Brass, 'KOSB'. Trews, No. 7 tartan. Black shoes, khaki gloves. *Pipers:* Highland pattern. *CB, B:* As soldiers, silver. Trews or kilt, Royal Stewart tartan. Footless stockings in red and black marl, plain red and black

...icing. White spats. White hair purse, two long ...lack tassels, badge as on cap but smaller, worn on ...lack belt. Bagpipe cover and ribbons in Royal ...tewart tartan; cords red, white, green, and blue. ...b: Strip of tartan; black buckles, left.

The Black Watch (Royal Highland Regiment); 42nd and 73rd Foot

Facings: Blue. *Bonnet*: Blue, red hackle above badge over left ear. *OSD*: Highland pattern, no CB. *B*: Brass, with cap badge in circular form. Trews and kilt in No 1 (42nd) tartan; brown leather Highland purse with silver regimental badge. Two dark-green bows with 8 in. ribbons on right of kilt, knife pleats to rear of kilt showing black lines. Cap badge: As soldiers' but gilt crown, scroll, thistles, sphinx; silver St Andrew with cross. Footless stockings in red and black marl with plain red and black dicing. Black brogue shoes. *SSD, Bandsmens', Drummers'*: Highland pattern. *CB*: Silver, St Andrew with cross. *B*: As officers. *ST*: Brass, 'BW'. Sporran badge, brass St Andrew with cross on thistles. Kilt, trews, stockings as officers. White Highland purse with five short black tassels, regimental badge, on white belt. *SB*: Strip of No. 1 tartan; black buckles, left. *Pipers*: Kilt, trews in Royal Stewart tartan. Bagpipe cords, cover and ribbons in No. 1 tartan. Otherwise as SSD.

Queen's Own Highlanders (Seaforth and Camerons); 72nd, 78th and 79th Foot

Facings: Buff and blue. *Glengarry*: Blue, scarlet toorie. Blue cut feather hackle on bonnet. *OSD*: Highland pattern. *CB*: Silver, elephant facing inwards under scrolls with 'ASSAYE'. *B*: As cap badge, without scroll. Kilt in No. 2 Mackenzie tartan (Seaforth sett). Trews in No. 4 (Cameron of Erracht) tartan. Silver sporran badge of crowned thistle. Footless stockings in red and white marl with plain red and white dicing. *SSD*: Highland pattern. *CB*: *B*: As officers. Kilt, trews, stockings, sporran badge; as officers. *ST*: Brass, 'QO' over arc 'HIGHLANDERS'. White spats for parades. Belt-plate bears silver St Andrew with cross between thistles over scroll with 'WATERLOO'. Black hair purse with two long white tassels, regimental badge, black belt. *Drummers', Bandsmens' SD*: As soldiers but kilt in No. 4 Erracht tartan, trews in No. 2 Mackenzie tartan. *Pipers*: As soldiers but kilt in No. 4, trews in No. 2 tartan; footless stockings in

Major, Royal Anglians, wearing the Temperate DPM combat dress and the new khaki beret with black patch behind the badge recently approved for wear by this regiment by the Army Dress Committee.

Left, a Sergeant Major instructor of the Small Arms School Corps, wearing his ranking and a small arms instructor's badge sewn to his khaki barrack dress jersey. *Right,* a Sergeant of the Royal Irish Rangers handles a 120mm anti-tank gun. Note the ranger-green chevrons on black backing, the bright green shamrock patch above them, and the brass shoulder titles IRISH RANGERS on ranger-green tape. (*Soldier Magazine*)

red and green marl with plain red and green dicing. Bagpipe cords, cover and ribbons in Mackenzie tartan. *SB:* Strips of tartan.

The Gordon Highlanders; 75th and 92nd Foot

Facings: Yellow. *Glengarry:* Blue; scarlet, blue and white dicing, scarlet toorie. *OSD:* Highland pattern. *CB:* Dark-bronze sphinx facing inwards on plinth inscribed 'EGYPT'. *B:* Brass, St Andrew's cross behind (top) sphinx and 'EGYPT', facing left; (bottom) tiger passant gardant over label with 'INDIA'. Surrounding these, a wreath of thistles in lower half and a scroll with 'GORDON HIGHLANDERS' in top half. Kilt, trews in No. 3 Gordon tartan. Knife pleats to back of kilt, each showing yellow line. Footless stockings in red and white marl with plain red and white dicing. Brown Highland purse with badge. Sporran badge, silver, a stag's head issuing from a coronet with a crowned label 'BYDAND' between the antler points, below he coronet a scroll with 'GORDON HIGHLANDERS'. Black brogue shoes. White spats for parade. *SSD, Bandsmens', Drummers', Pipers'*: Highland pattern. *CB*: Silver, tigers passant gardant, facing inwards. *ST*: Brass, in arc, 'GORDONS'. Buttons, sporran badge as officers. White hair purse, two long black tassels, from white belt; no badge. Bagpipe cords, cover and ribbons in No. 3 tartan. *SB*: Strip of No. 3 tartan.

The Argyll and Sutherland Highlanders (Princess Louise's); 91st and 93rd Foot

Facings: Yellow. *Glengarry*: Blue; scarlet and white dicing, scarlet toorie. *OSD*: Highland pattern. *CB*: Dark bronze, within two circles of laurels a boar's head facing inwards over a scroll with 'NE OBLIVISCA RIS', in the outside ring a wild cat rampant gardant facing inwards above a scroll with 'SANS PEUR'. *B*: Brass, as collar badge but surmounted by coronet. Kilt, trews in No. 1 (42nd) tartan; sporran in brown leather with badge: under a coronet the reversed, entwined cypher 'L', to the left a boar's head looking left, to the right a wild cat looking left, all silver. Footless stockings in red and white marl with plain red and white dicing. Black brogue shoes. White spats for parade. *SSD, Bandsmens' Drummers', Pipers*: Highland pattern; kilt, trews, stockings as officers. Two bright-green $1\frac{1}{2}$-in. silk rosettes on right of kilt with 6-in. trailing ribbons and bright-green embroidery. Double-fringed end to kilt; box pleats to rear, each showing black line. *CB*: As officers but silver. *ST*: Brass 'A&SH'. Buttons, sporran badge, as officers. White hair purse with six short black tassels, from black belt; officers have badger-mask decoration to lids of purses. Bagpipe cords and cover in Black Watch tartan, ribbons in Sutherland tartan. *J*: Officers, grey.

The Queen's Division

The Queen's Regiment; 2nd, 3rd, 31st, 35th, 50th, 57th, 70th, 77th, 97th, 107th Foot

Facings: Blue. *SH*: Dark-blue flaps, body and peak, scarlet piping, two buttons. *Bt*: Blue. *OSD: CB*: 8-point star, behind this the plume of Roussillon, all silver; in centre of star a gold Garter; in centre of Garter, the silver prancing horse of Kent facing inwards. *B*: Brass; 8-point star, the top point obscured by crown; within circular centrepiece, lamb with halo and banner of St George, facing left. *SSD*: As officers. *ST*: Brass, 'QUEEN'S'. Sgts and above wear *L*: 1st Bn, 2nd Bn, dark-blue; 3rd Bn, Royal Dutch orange. *SB*: Dark-blue, brass plate.

The Royal Regiment of Fusiliers; 5th, 6th, 7th and 20th Foot

Facings: Blue. *DC*: Royal, worn by officers and WOs only. *Bt*: Blue, red-over white cut feather hackle behind badge. *OSD: CB*: Flaming grenade in gold, bearing St George and dragon in wreath, silver, facing left. *B*: Brass; within crowned Garter a stag with collar and chain facing left. *ST*: Brass, 'RRF'. *SSD*: As officers. *SB*: Equal stripes crimson, yellow, crimson; brown buckles, left.

The Royal Anglian Regiment; 9th, 10th, 12th, 16th, 17th, 44th, 48th, 56th and 58th Foot

Facings: Blue. *SH*: Dark-blue body and flaps, scarlet peak, gold body piping, two buttons. *Bt*: Khaki, black cloth patch behind badge. *OSD: CB*: Exactly as cap badge. *B*: Brass; a tiger, passant gardant within oval laurel wreath, facing left. Cap button has tiger and wreath in silver. *SSD*: As officers but without silver on cap button. *ST*: Brass, 'ROYAL' over 'ANGLIAN'. *L*: 1st Bn, sgts and above, yellow; 2nd Bn, officers and WOs only, black; 3rd Bn, sgts and above, purple; 4th Bn, sgts and above, grey, red and black. *SB*: Dark-blue, central scarlet band with narrow yellow stripe, brass plate with cap badge. *J*: Sometimes dark-green.

The King's Division

The King's Own Royal Border Regiment; 4th, 34th and 55th Foot

Facings: Blue. *SH*: Blue body, red flaps and peak, gold-piped flaps and body for officers, two buttons, embroidered badge. *Bt*: Blue, red diamond patch behind badge, which is embroidered for officers. *OSD: CB*: Silver lion gardant passant, facing inwards. *B*: Brass; Chinese dragon under 'CHINA'. Dragon only on cap button. Gold glider badge at top of right arm. Malacca canes with silver tip and silver knob with regimental badge. *SSD:* As officers. *ST:* Brass, 'KING'S OWN' in convex arc above 'BORDER'. Yellow glider badge at top of right arm. *SB:* Blue, $\frac{3}{4}$-in. central gold stripe, brass plate with cap badge. *C:* Kendal-green. Officers wear green, slip-on shoulder tabs on combat and fatigue dress with plain cloth ranking and ST as above in black cotton. Yellow glider badge and ST worn on J by officers.

The King's Regiment; 8th, 63rd and 96th Foot

Facings: Deep green. *SH:* Maroon, no peak, dark-green tip, badge embroidered gold and silver on dark-green. *Bt:* Blue, scarlet patch $1\frac{7}{8}$-in. square behind badge. *OSD: CB:* As cap badge, silver horse facing inwards. *B:* Brass; fleur-de-lys. In shirt-sleeve order officers may wear blue-grey shirt,

Royal Artillery gunners firing the 105mm Light Gun, 1972. Some of this group wear the normal puttees, others retain black polished web anklets of '37-pattern. At the time of writing many artillerymen wear the DPM combat cap instead of the dark blue beret; they retain the regimental cap badge. (*Soldier* Magazine)

brass ranking and ST. *SSD:* As officers. *ST:* Brass 'KING'S' in concave arc. Silver buckle plate with cap badge or '37-pattern buckle. *L:* Sgts and above, green. *SB:* Dark-green, central $\frac{5}{8}$-in. maroon stripe; brown buckles, left. *J:* Officers green V-neck, detachable epaulettes, brass ranking and ST.

The Prince of Wales's Own Regiment of Yorkshire; 14th and 15th Foot

Facings: White. *DC:* Blue, blue band, scarlet piping. *SH:* Maroon flaps and peak, buff body piped black, two buttons. *Bt:* Blue. *OSD: CB:* 8-point gold star, in centre black disc within gold wreath with silver rose. *B:* Brass, below Prince of Wales's plumes, coronet and motto 'ICH DIEN' the springing horse (as cap badge). *SSD: CB:* As officers but silver rose extends out to gold wreath. *ST:* Brass, 'PWO'. *SB:* Maroon, central $\frac{1}{2}$-in. yellow stripe, $\frac{1}{2}$-in. black edges; black buckles, left. *J:* Dark-green.

he Green Howards (Alexandra, Princess of Wales's Own Yorkshire Regiment); 19th Foot

acings: Grass-green. *DC:* Blue, blue band, scarlet iping. *SH:* Grass-green body, dark-blue peak and aps, gold-piped flaps and body, embroidered adge, two buttons. *Bt:* Blue; officers, embroidered adge on green backing; soldiers, 2-in. green quare patch behind badge. *OSD: CB:* Silver, as ap badge without scroll. *B:* Brass, as cap badge. lap buttons have silver badge, no scroll. *L:* Grass-reen. *SSD:* As officers; no silver on cap buttons; *L,* gts and above only. *ST:* Brass, 'GREEN' above HOWARDS'. Officers' buckle plate, silver with XIX' in laurel wreath; soldiers', brass with cap adge. *SB:* Grass-green, narrow white central tripe; brown buckles, left. *J:* Officers, dark-green J-neck, green epaulettes with brass ranking and T. *King Olav Coy.:* Rifle coys. compete for title nnually. Silver badge on green backing on upper ight arm, Royal Norwegian cypher, crowned 'O' on 'V'. Green backing to badges and chevrons for other ranks. These distinctions worn, though as yet officially unapproved.

The Royal Irish Rangers; 27th (Inniskilling), 83rd and 87th Foot

Facings: Piper-green. *Bonnet:* Piper-green ('Ranger'-green), badge over left eye, dark-green cut feather hackle. *OSD:* Piper-green trousers, black Highland shoes, brown gloves; black shoulder-belt and pouch instead of Sam Browne. *CB:* Silver, a three-towered castle, flag flying to right, beneath label 'INNISKILLING'. *B:* Black; as cap badge without scroll, on shamrock sprigs within scalloped ring. Rank badges black. *SSD:* Piper-green trousers. *CB:* Silver, as officers but single casting. *ST:* Brass, 'IRISH' above 'RANGERS' in two arcs. *B:* As officers. Black belt, silver plate. Black gloves. Rank, skill-at-arms and

1st Coldstream Guards in Norway, 1969. Part of the regular training of the UK Allied Mobile Force is carried out in Norway. The Bergen Rucksack seen here is the standard version; a narrower pattern, easier for use by skiers, has been developed. Note the GPMG mounted on the sledge. (COI)

trade badges in piper-green on black backing. *Bandsmen, Drummers, Buglers and Pipers:* Oversize bonnet badges. Pipers have silver buttons, saffron serge kilt, piper-green stockings. *SB:* Piper-green, plain silver clasp. *C:* Piper-green.

The Queen's Lancashire Regiment; 30th, 40th, 47th, 59th, 81st and 82nd Foot

Facings: Blue. *SH:* Maroon body, peak and flaps, black tip, two buttons, embroidered badge for officers. *Bt:* Blue, diamond-shape primrose patch behind badge. *OSD:* Cap badge gold with red enamel rose under crown. *CB:* Red and gold rose over gold scroll with 'QUEEN'S LANCASHIRE'. *B:* Brass, with rose. Whangee cane with silver tip and knob with regimental badge. Olive-green slip-on shoulder tabs with cloth ranking and maroon 'LANCASHIRE' with combat, fatigue and barrack dress. *SSD:* As officers, CB & B in brass. *ST:* Brass, 'LANCASHIRES'. Silver belt-plate with cap badge. Sgts and above, maroon *L*, double cord, three knots. *SB:* Maroon, silver '37-pattern buckle.

The Duke of Wellington's Regiment (West Riding); 33rd and 76th Foot

Facings: Scarlet. *DC:* Blue, blue band, scarlet piping, scarlet backing to badge. *SH:* Blue body, peak and flaps, gold-piped body, metal badge on scarlet backing. *Bt:* Blue, scarlet backing to badge. *OSD: CB:* Gold Indian elephant facing inwards, silver howdah. *B:* Brass; elephant facing left within peripheral inscription 'DUKE OF WELLINGTON'S' (top) and 'WEST RIDING REGT' (bottom). No inscription on cap buttons. *SSD:* As officers, CB all brass. *ST:* Brass, 'DWR'. Sgts and above, red *L*. Belt-plate silver, with cap badge.

The Prince of Wales's Division

The Devonshire and Dorset Regiment; 11th, 39th and 54th Foot

Facings: Grass-green. *DC:* Blue, blue band, scarlet piping. *SH:* Blue flaps and peak, grass-green body piped gold for officers, two buttons. *Bt:* Blue. *OSD: CB:* Small versions of cap badge, sphinx facing

inwards. *B:* Brass; Prince of Wales's plume, coronet and motto, silver on cap buttons. *L:* Grass-green. *SSD:* As officers, no silver crest on cap buttons. *ST:* Brass 'DEVON' in convex arc over '&' over 'DORSET' in concave arc. *L:* Sgts and above, grass-green. All ranks wear strip 1914– French Croix de Guerre ribbon 2 in. from top each sleeve. *SB:* Grass-green, tawny orange centre stripe; brown buckles, left.

The Cheshire Regiment; 22nd Foot

Facings: Buff. *DC:* Blue, blue band, scarlet piping. *SH:* Blue flaps, peak, and buff-piped body, buff tip, two buttons, metal badge. *Bt:* Blue. *OSD: CB:* Matt bronze acorn within oakleaf sprigs. Cap badge smaller than soldiers' with green backing to acorn. *B:* Brass; 8-point star, in centre circular band with 'THE CHESHIRE REGIMENT' surrounding oakleaves and acorn as cap badge. *SSD:* As officers but CB have silver acorn, brass acorn-cup and leaves. *ST:* Brass, 'CHESHIRE' in concave arc. *L:* Red, sgts and above. *SB:* Cerise and buff, circular clasp with '22'.

The Royal Welch Fusiliers; 23rd Foot

Facings: Blue. *DC:* Royal, officers and WOs only. *Bt:* Blue, white cut-feather hackle. Officers' badge embroidered gold grenade, silver Welsh dragon, red backing to flames. *OSD:* Dark-bronze cap badge, as soldiers. *CB:* Dark-bronze flaming grenade with rampant Welsh dragon facing inwards. *B:* Brass, Welsh dragon facing left. *SSD: CB:* Small plain flaming grenades, brass. *ST:* Brass, 'RWF'. *SB:* Equal $1\frac{1}{4}$-in. maroon and blue stripes; black buckles, left. All ranks wear 'Flash' from rear of SD jacket collar: five black swallow-tail ribbons about 9 in. long × 2 in. wide.

The Royal Regiment of Wales; 24th/41st Foot

Facings: Grass-green. *Bt:* Blue, grass-green badge backing. *OSD: CB:* Silver, within wreath of Immortelles a rampant, winged Welsh dragon facing inwards. *B:* Brass, dragon facing left. On jersey, black cloth ranking and 'RRW' on epaulette. 'Everleigh Star' rank badges, and large field-officers' crowns. *SSD:* As officers. *ST:* Brass, 'RRW'. WOs' ranking worn on grass-green backing. *SB:* Grass-green, broad white centre stripe thinly edged red; silver buckle-plate of dragon within Immortelle wreath. *J:* Regimental green.

The Gloucestershire Regiment; 28th and 61st Foot

Facings: Primrose yellow. *DC:* Blue, blue band, scarlet piping. *SH:* Dark-blue peak, scarlet-piped dark-blue body and flaps, primrose tip, two buttons, embroidered badge. *Bt:* Blue. On all headgear this regiment wears small silver badge on back, sphinx within wreath, in addition to front cap badge. *OSD:* Dark-bronze cap badge as soldiers'. *CB:* Dark-bronze, sphinx between laurel wreaths, facing inwards. *B:* Dark-bronze; lion on crown over interlocked 'G' and 'R' within laurel wreath.

Disbandment parade of the Cameronians (The Scottish Rifles) on 14 May 1968. The dark-green Glengarry has a black toorie and the silver badge of the Lowland Brigade, as it then was; the tartan trews were in No. 6 (Douglas), and buttons and embellishments were black. The Sam Browne is seen here in an unusual configuration, with both braces worn, vertically. (*Soldier* Magazine)

SSD: As officers, but CB silver. *ST:* Brass, 'GLOSTER' in concave arc. *SB:* Dark-blue; red 1/5th-in. centre stripe, flanked by yellow 1/10th-in. stripes ½ in. from belt edges; brown buckles, left. *J:* Black, with black shoulder straps and brass buttons for officers. All ranks wear U.S. Presidential Citation patch at top of arm: small light-blue rectangle edged gold.

Cloth shoulder patches identifying army, corps, division or brigade in the Second World War manner are no longer worn on No. 1, No. 2, No. 4 or No. 6 Dress, and are only rarely seen nowadays on combat dress; they are practically restricted to unit notice-boards, vehicles, stationery, etc. Some are reproduced here; recent re-organization of BAOR divisions may soon lead to their complete disappearance. *Top left:* 1st British Corps, BAOR—silver spearhead on red diamond. *Top centre:* 2nd Division (in BAOR)—crossed silver keys on black square. *Top right:* 4th Division (in BAOR)—black square, red disc with upper left quarter separated. *Bottom left:* 1st Division (in BAOR)—white triangle outlined red. *Bottom centre:* 3rd Division (in Strategic Reserve, UK)—three red triangles surrounding white triangle, all edged black. Also illustrated here, *extreme top right*, is the yellow glider badge worn on the sleeve by all ranks of the King's Own Royal Border Regiment and the Staffordshire Regiment in commemoration of gliderborne operations in Sicily, July 1943. Below this is the shoulder patch of Land Forces Hong Kong—a gold dragon on red-over-black-over-red stripes.

The Worcestershire and Sherwood Foresters Regiment; 29th, 36th, 45th and 95th Foot

Facings: Lincoln-green. *DC:* Blue, blue band, scarlet piping. *Bt:* Blue, Lincoln-green badge backing. *OSD:* Cap badge as illustrated but dark-blue enamel backing to central device. *CB:* As cap badge but smaller; stags face inwards. *B:* Brass, with cap badge. *L:* Lincoln-green. *SSD:* As officers, no blue in cap badge. *ST:* Brass, 'WORCESTERS' in arc above '&' above 'FORESTERS' in arc. *L:* Lincoln-green, right shoulder, sgts and above. *SB:* Lincoln-green, 1/3rd-in. maroon central stripe; brown buckles, left. *C:* Lincoln-green.

The Royal Hampshire Regiment; 37th and 67th Foot

Facings: Yellow. *SH:* Blue body, flaps and peak, yellow tip and flap-piping, two buttons, em-broidered badge. *Bt:* Blue. *OSD:* Cap badge: 8 point silver star, gold crown with red cushion obscuring top point; blue enamel Garter around red, gold and green rose; below Garter, blue scroll with gold 'ROYAL HAMPSHIRE'. *CB:* Rose in laurel wreath in red, green and gold. *B:* Brass, tiger over rose within laurel wreath. *SB:* Black with stripes of yellow, red, green, mauve; bronze three clasp buckle. *SSD:* Cap badge as illustrated—silver tiger over gold rose in crowned laurel wreath, gold scroll with 'ROYAL HAMPSHIRE'. *CB, B:* Brass, as officers. *ST:* Brass, 'R.HAMPSHIRE' in concave arc. Silver belt-plate with cap badge. *SB:* As officers but different arrangement of stripes. *J:* Black.

The Staffordshire Regiment (The Prince of Wales's); 38th, 64th, 80th and 98th Foot

Facings: Yellow. *DC:* Blue, blue band, scarlet piping, buff badge backing. *SH:* Blue peak, gold-piped blue body and flaps, two buttons, em-broidered badge. *Bt:* Blue, buff badge backing. *OSD: CB:* Gold, crowned Staffordshire knot; in centre silver Prince of Wales's plumes and scroll, gold coronet; buff 'Holland cloth' backing. *B:* Brass, with collar badge. Gold glider badge top of right arm. *L:* Black, left shoulder. *SSD:* As officers'. *ST:* Brass, 'STAFFORDS'. Yellow thread glider badge. *L:* Sgts and above, black. *SB:* Black, 76 mm wide; black buckles, left.

1 **General, Tropical Service Dress**
2 **Major, Scots Guards, No. 2 Dress**
3 **Corporal, 10th Gurkha Rifles, Tropical Parade Dress**

1

2

3

A

1 **Colour Bearer, Royal Hampshire Regt.**
2 **Sergeant, 5th Royal Inniskilling Dragoon Guards, No. 2 Dress**
3 **Corporal, Royal Hussars, No. 2 Dress**

B

ANGUS McBRIDE

1 Lance Corporal, Royal Military Police
2 Company Sergeant Major, Royal Scots
3 Staff Sergeant, King's Troop RHA
  Winter Stable Dress

ANGUS McBRIDE

C

1 **Captain, WRAC, Service Dress**
2 **Lieutenant, King's Regiment, Summer Barrack Dress**
3 **Lieutenant, QARANC, No. 2 Dress**

ANGUS McBRIDE

1   **Lieutenant Pilot, AAC, Flying Clothing**
2   **Radio Operator, Light Infantry,**
     Temperate DPM Combat Dress
3   **Corporal, 2nd RTR, Combat Dress**

ANGUS McBRIDE

E

1 **Gurkha Rifleman, Olive Drab Tropical Combat Dress**
2 **Infantryman, Tropical DPM Combat Dress**
3 **Private, Royal Anglian Regt, Arctic Combat Dress**

F

ANGUS McBRIDE

Northern Ireland:
1 Riot Gear
2 Ammunition Technician, RAOC
3 Royal Regt of Fusiliers,
  Summer Dress

ANGUS McBRIDE

G

1 RSM, Gordon Highlanders, No. 2 Dress
2 Parachute Regt, Battle Jumping Order
3 Possible Service Dress, 1980s

H

Duke of Edinburgh's Royal Regiment (Berkshire and Wiltshire); 49th, 62nd, 66th and 99th Foot

Facings: Blue. *DC:* Royal, red badge backing. *SH:* Blue body piped scarlet, blue flaps and peak, two buttons, embroidered badge. *Bt:* Blue, red badge backing. *OSD: CB:* As cap badge, dragons facing inwards, on red backing. *B:* Brass; Prince of Wales's plumes, coronet and scroll. *ST:* Brass, 'DUKE OF EDINBURGH'S' in convex arc over 'ROYAL REGIMENT' in arc. *L:* Blue. *SSD:* As officers, but ST brass lettering on rectangular silver plate. *L:* Sgts and above, blue. *SB:* Blue, two narrow scarlet bands; brown buckles, left.

The Light Division

The Light Infantry; 13th, 32nd, 46th, 51st, 53rd, 68th, 85th, 105th and 106th Foot

Facings: Blue. *DC:* Rifle-green, rifle-green band and piping. *SH:* Rifle-green, silver horn badge worn at front on semi-spherical rifle-green boss. *Bt:* Rifle-green. Badge has red backing showing between horn and cords. *OSD: CB:* Dark-bronze bugle horn, mouthpiece inwards. *B:* Brass with cap badge. Black ranking (black cloth on jersey). Brown Sam Browne, brass fittings. Brown gloves. Black Highland shoes. Rifle-green whistle-cord on left shoulder. *SSD: CB:* Silver, as officers. *ST:* Silver bugle horn, mouthpiece to front, over scroll

Skill-at-arms badges in white on khaki, or in some cases in colour of regimental chevrons, are worn on the right sleeve. Trade or employment badges, usually in white on khaki, are worn by corporals and below, on the upper sleeve. The representative examples illustrated are, *top row, left to right:* AAC Air Gunner's breast badge—yellow crowned ring and G, light blue wing, dark blue ground; Bomb Disposal unit RE—yellow and blue on red; A Class Tradesman; Artificer REME—khaki, worn above chevrons or below warrant badge; Radar Mechanic REME. *Bottom row, left to right:* Gun Layer; Sub-Machine Gun Marksman; Mortarman; Bugler (LI); Driver.

'LIGHT INFANTRY'. All badges rifle-green on maize. Green gloves. WOs and senior NCOs wear whistle-cord as officers. WOIIs and sgts wear scarlet infantry sashes over left shoulder, knot at right hip; and silver whistle-chain from lion's-head boss at V-point of collar with whistle tucked into belt on right of buckle. *SB:* Rifle-green; black buckles, left.

The Royal Green Jackets; 43rd and 52nd Foot, King's Royal Rifle Corps, Rifle Brigade

Facing: Black. *DC:* Rifle-green, rifle-green band and piping. *SH:* Rifle-green, two buttons; silver horn badge worn at front on rifle-green semi-spherical boss. *Bt:* Rifle-green. *OSD: CB:* Dark-bronze bugle horn, mouthpiece inwards. *B:* Black, crowned bugle, mouthpiece to right; four front buttons spherical. *ST:* Black, bugle over Gothic 'RGJ'. Black gloves, black Highland shoes. Black crossbelt and pouch; silver crossbelt badge, larger version of cap badge; pouch badge, silver bugle horn, mouthpiece to right. *SSD: CB, B, ST:* As officers—only WOs have spherical buttons. Black belt, brass plate with cap badge. Chevrons black,

Sergeant Piper, Royal Highland Fusiliers, in No. 2 Dress, Parade Order, 1967. There have been some uniform changes since the date of this photograph, but colour details are as follows: Blue Glengarry, red toorie, silver Highland Brigade cap badge—on St Andrew's Cross a stag's mask above a scroll with 'CUIDICH'NRIGH', all on black silk square. Gold and silver collar badges, brass buttons, brass bagpipe badge on red backing, red sash. Erskine tartan kilt, bagpipe cover and ribbons. Silver sporran top, white hair purse with three long black tassels. Green and red marl stockings with plain red and green dicing overstriped red and green on opposite colours; white spats, Erskine tartan garter tabs, black Highland shoes. (*Soldier* Magazine)

retaining its loose cut, ribbed woollen cuffs an crutch-strap, but in standard DPM camouflage. I will probably be worn with DPM trousers. Befor the recent disbandment of the airborne brigad structure, the following distinctions were worn:

	$2\frac{3}{4}$in. square patch on smock sleeve	No. 2 Dress Lanyard
Brigade HQ	Light-blue over maroon	Light-blue and maroon
1st Bn.	Red	Red
2nd Bn.	Blue	Blue
3rd Bn.	Green	Green
7 Para RHA	Scarlet over blue	As parent corps
216 Para Signals Sqn.	White over blue	As parent corps
63 Para Sqn. RCT	Diagonally halved blue and gold	As parent corps
23 Para Fld. Ambulance	Cherry over blue over yellow	As parent corps
16 Para Heavy Drop Coy. RAOC / 16 Para Ordnance Field Park	Red, blue, red vertical stripes	As parent corps
16 Para Workshops	Blue and scarlet	As parent corps

The Brigade of Gurkhas

Officers in this Brigade wear black patent-leather shoulder belts (crimson for Gurkha Engineers) for parades. The belts have silver fittings—a breast badge, a lion's-head mask (ram's head for 2nd GR), chains and whistle. The black pouch bears a small silver badge. All fittings for Gurkha Engineers are gold. In No. 2 Dress, Gurkha soldiers may wear the khaki slouch hat with khaki turban and badge on the left side; or the black 'pill-box' Kilmarnock with toorie according to regiment and frontal badge; or their rifle-green beret. Queen's Gurkha Officers wear a strip of lace under their shoulder ranking; this is $\frac{1}{2}$-in. dark-green lace with

edged gold all round, on rifle-green backing. *L:* Officers and WOs only, green and black. *SB:* Rifle-green; black buckles, left.

The Parachute Regiment
Facings: Maroon. *Bt:* Maroon. *OSD: CB:* Officers and WOIs, as cap badge but dark-bronze, lions face inwards. *B:* Brass, as cap badge. *SSD: CB:* As officers, silver. *ST:* Brass, 'PARACHUTE' in arc over 'REGIMENT' in arc.

Instead of DPM Temperature or Tropical Combat Dress the regiment wear the Denison Smock—a post-war development of the wartime garment—and Olive Drab Lightweight Trousers. A new smock is planned to replace the Denison,

$\frac{1}{8}$-in. red centre stripe flanked by 1/16-in. green and $\frac{1}{8}$-in. black stripes. British officers wear either No. 1 or No. 2 Dress caps, the latter with black chinstraps; berets; or side hats with a small badge mounted on a semi-spherical cord boss at the front, though 1 in.–1$\frac{1}{4}$ in. diameter.

2nd King Edward VII's Own Gurkha Rifles (The Sirmoor Rifles)

Facings: Scarlet. *DC:* Rifle-green, black piping, diced red and black band two squares deep, badge worn on upper red square; officers only. Badge mounted on scarlet boss on all officers' headgear. *FSH:* Rifle-green body, peak and tip, two buttons, officer's badge boss top front. Piped tip: black for WOs, three red stripes for c/sgts and sgts, two for cpls, one for l/cpls. Soldier's cap badge worn on side. *Bt:* Rifle-green. *Cap-badge:* Prince of Wales's plume, scroll and coronet, worn on red backing, silver for officers, black for ORs. *Kilmarnock:* Black toorie, dice band as *DC*; officers wear black badges without backing. *Slouch hat. badge:* Soldiers' style, on piece black and red dice two squares wide by three high, two black squares to front, on left of turban. *OSD:* Scarlet 1/10-in. piping around collar as far as step. *B:* Black ball, Edwardian crown over entwined 'ERI' over crossed kukris, hilts and edges down. *ST:* Black, '2GR'. Ranking black on scarlet backing. Black gloves and Highland shoes. *L:* Black, left shoulder. Off parade, blackthorn walking stick. *SSD:* English. Ranking, black on scarlet. *B:* Semi-raised, as

AAC Air Gunner checking helicopter-mounted anti-tank missile system; note pale blue beret, and AAC shoulder patch and white chevrons on olive-green flying suit, and knife worn hilt downwards on thigh. (*Soldier* Magazine)

above without crown. *L:* Sgts and above, black, left arm. *ST:* As above. *SB:* Central green band $\frac{7}{8}$ in. wide flanked by $\frac{1}{4}$-in. scarlet bands and black $\frac{3}{4}$-in. outer edges; black buckles, right.

6th Queen Elizabeth's Own Gurkha Rifles

Facings: Black. *DC:* Rifle-green, black piping, officers only. *SH:* Rifle-green piped black, two buttons, black badge boss at front. *Bt:* Rifle-green. *Cap-badge:* Two kukris in saltire, hilts and edges down, over '6', the whole ensigned with the crown,

Pioneer Sergeant, Royal Highland Fusiliers, in No. 2 Dress, 1967. Tradition requires every infantry battalion Pioneer Sergeant in the Army to wear a full beard and moustache. No other officer or soldier may wear a beard except for special medical reasons. The Glengarry dicing is red, white, and green; the axes badge is outlined red, on a khaki patch. The SD jacket is of Highland pattern, worn with trews in No. 5A (Mackenzie) tartan. The medal ribbons include an early Africa Star, showing that this long-service NCO fought in the early stages of the 1940–43 Africa campaign. (*Soldier* Magazine)

all in silver. *Kilmarnock:* Scarlet toorie. *Slouch ha* Badge as above, left. *OSD:* Side hat, beret and S cap badge, as above in miniature black bc (approx. 1 in. across). *B:* Black, with cap badge. silver on upper arm, cap badge of 14th/20th Th King's Hussars. *SSD:* English. Ranking, black c rifle-green. *ST:* Black, '6GR'. *L.* Rifle-green an black. Pipers wear a round silver brooch at th shoulder to hold the dark-green scarf, the pierce centre showing the cap badge.

7th Duke of Edinburgh's Own Gurkha Rifle

Facings: Black. *DC:* Rifle-green, black piping officers only *SH:* As 6th GR. *Bt:* Rifle-green. *Cap badge:* Two kukris, points up, hilts crossed i saltire, edges inwards; between blades '7' below entwined, reversed cypher 'P', below coronet, all i silver. *Kilmarnock:* Black toorie. *Slouch hat:* Badge a

above, left. *OSD:* No. 1 and No. 2 Dress cap badges as above, miniature, on black boss. *Bt:* Full size badge, no boss. *B:* Black, with cap badge. *L:* Rifle-green and black. *SSD:* English. Ranking, black on rifle-green. Cap-badge, buttons as above. *ST:* Black, '7GR'. *L:* As above. Pipers and drummers wear trews, scarf and plaid in No. 6 Douglas tartan, for parade; pipers have heavy silver shoulder brooch, crowned Maltese cross within laurel wreath.

10th Princess Mary's Own Gurkha Rifles

Facings: Black. *DC:* Rifle-green, black piping, officers only. *SH:* As 6th GR. *Bt:* Rifle-green. *Cap-badge:* Bugle horn stringed interlaced with a kukri fessewise, the blade to the sinister, above the kukri the cypher of HRH Princess Mary (The Princess Royal) and below it the numeral '10', all in silver. *Kilmarnock:* Black toorie. *Slouch hat:* Badge as above, left. *OSD:* No. 1 and No. 2 Dress cap badges as above, miniature, on black boss. *B:* Black, with cap badge. *L:* Black. *SSD:* English. Ranking, black on rifle-green. *B:* As above. *ST:* Black, '10GR'. *L:* Black. Pipers and drummers wear trews, scarf and plaid in No. 8 Hunting Stewart tartan for parades, pipers with shoulder brooch as 6th GR but with central cap badge of 10th GR.

Gurkha Engineers

Facings: Blue. *DC:* Rifle-green, black piping,

Uniforms of regular and Territorial Highland regiments, 1968: from left: **(1) Liverpool Scottish (TAVR):** blue Glengarry, red toorie, blue hackle, silver badge. Kilt in No. 9 (Forbes) tartan, black purse, lovat-green stockings, red garter tabs. **(2) Pipe Major, Cameron Highlanders, No. 1 Dress:** blue Glengarry, red toorie, grey feathers, red sash. Piper-green doublet, silver lace and badges, black and silver dirk on right hip, grey hair purse with two white tassels. Kilt and plaid in No. 4 (Erracht) tartan. Red and green marl stockings with plain dicing, black shoes. **(3) Sergeant, 2nd Bn, Queen's Own Highlanders, No. 2 Dress, Parade Order:** blue Glengarry, red toorie, silver badge, deep-blue tuft. Red sash. Trews in No. 4 tartan. **(4) Drum Major, Argyll & Sutherland Highlanders, Full Dress:** black feather bonnet, white plume, 3-row red and white diced band. Piper-green doublet, red sash, yellow drum major's sash with silver embroidery; kilt and plaid in No. 1A tartan—as Black Watch but lighter green. Red and white stockings, plain dicing; black and silver dirk on right hip. **(5) Private, Lovat Scouts (TAVR), No. 1 Dress:** Blue bonnet and toorie, silver badge, blue jacket with silver embellishments; trews in No. 19 (Hunting Fraser) tartan. **(6) Piper, Seaforth Highlanders, No. 1 Dress:** blue Glengarry, red toorie, silver badge; piper-green doublet with silver buttons and badges; kilt, plaid and stockings in No. 2 (Mackenzie) tartan. **(7) L/Cpl, Black Watch, No. 2 Dress:** blue bonnet, red toorie and hackle; khaki jacket, shirt and tie; black Highland purse with silver badge; kilt in No. 1 (42nd) tartan; red and black stockings, red garter tabs. **(8) Private, Gordon Highlanders, combat dress with kilt:** khaki bonnet and toorie, silver badge on tartan patch; olive drab jacket; regimental kilt, lovat-green stockings, red garter tabs, khaki puttees; no purse; '58-pattern equipment. **(9) Drummer, Liverpool Scottish (TAVR), Full Dress:** black bonnet, white plume, white dicing, silver badge; piper-green doublet with silver embellishments; kilt and plaid in No. 9 tartan; red and black stockings, red garter tabs. (*Soldier* Magazine)

officers only. *SH:* As Royal Engineers. *Cap-badge:* Two kukris in saltire, blades up, edges out, in silver, below gold flaming grenade; over hilts a scroll with 'UBIQUE' in gold. *Kilmarnock:* Yellow 1-in. band, yellow toorie. *Slouch hat:* Badge as above, left. *OSD:* No. 1 and No. 2 Dress cap badges as above,

The new parachutist's smock and helmet. The smock, in DPM camouflage, will replace the Denison smock but retains many of its design features. The lightweight helmet gives improved ballistic and impact protection. (Directorate of Clothing & Textiles)

The sniper suit, with built-in hood and camouflage loops, in the familiar DPM finish. (Directorate of Clothing & Textiles)

miniature, on dark-blue boss. *ST:* Black, 'GE'. *B:* Brass, with cap badge. *CB:* As cap badge. *SSD:* As officers. Pipers wear scarf in No. 24 McLecce tartan for parade, with silver shoulder brooch with central circular belt bearing 'HOLD FAST', and within the pierced centre a bull's head between lances.

Gurkha Signals

Facings: Black. *Cap-badge:* Gold crown over silver Mercury over crossed silver kukris, blades up, edges in, over gold scroll with 'CERTA CITO', silver bee superimposed on centre of scroll. *SH:* As Royal Signals but black buttons. *Kilmarnock:* Dark-blue toorie. *Slouch hat:* Badge as above, left, on backing of Grant tartan. *OSD: CB:* As cap badge, Mercury facing inwards. *ST:* Black, 'GURKHA' over 'SIGNALS'. *B:* Black, with cap badge. *SSD:*

English. As officers'; ranking black on blue. Pipers on parade wear scarf in No. 15 Red Grant tartan with figured silver shoulder brooch bearing in centre belt with 'STAND FAST', within the pierced centre a flaming volcano, around the belt thistle heads and leaves.

Gurkha Transport Regiment

Facings: White. *Cap-badge:* 8-point silver star with scroll with 'GURKHA TRANSPORT REGIMENT', upper part of scroll becoming gold laurel wreath; superimposed crossed kukris, hilts down, edges out, with silver blades and gold hilts; below gold crowned 'EIIR'. *SH:* Indigo body piped black, white tip, indigo flaps and peak, two black buttons. *Kilmarnock:* Back toorie. *Slouch hat:* Badge as above, left. *SD: CB:* As above. *ST:* Black,

GTR'. *B:* Brass, with cap badge minus star. *SSD:* s officers'. Pipers wear scarf of No. 16 McDuff artan on parade.

*   *   *

pecial Air Service Regiment

Facings: Cambridge blue. *Bt:* Beige with dark-blue patch bearing embroidered silver dagger badge with light-blue wings and scroll with motto 'WHO DARES WINS', all parts outlined red. This s worn in place of No. 1 and No. 2 Dress caps and ide hat by all ranks. *OSD: CB:* Silver dagger, gold wings and scroll. *B:* Silver, with cap badge. *SSD:* As officers, with *ST:* Black, 'SAS'. Ranking, black on pompadour blue. Combat dress is normally the DPM windproof smock and DPM field cap, with Olive Drab trousers.

Army Air Corps

Facings: Cambridge blue. *Bt:* Light-blue with square dark blue patch behind badge. *OSD:* RAC-

pattern. *CB:* The eagle of the cap badge, facing inwards. *B:* Brass, with eagle. *SSD:* As officers. White belt, brass plate with cap badge. Senior NCOs wear light blue eagle with dark blue edging between the crown and chevrons.

Royal Corps of Transport

Facings: White. *DC:* Blue, blue band, white piping. *SH:* Blue body, flaps, and peak all piped yellow, white tip, two buttons. *Bt:* Blue. *CB:* As cap badge. *B:* Brass, with 8-point star enclosing crown. *ST:* Soldiers only, brass, 'RCT'. *L:* Dark blue, left shoulder. WOIs' warrant badges outlined yellow. Members of the corps engaged in movement of personnel wear red brassards on the upper left sleeve with (old pattern) a yellow waggon wheel, or

Soldiers of 1st Bn, The Staffordshire Regiment waiting to board an RAF Puma helicopter during an exercise. They wear DPM combat dress and '58-pattern equipment. Visible among their equipment are radios with aerials collapsed, a Carl Gustav AT-launcher, and belts for the GPMG. (*Soldier Magazine*)

ellow 'MOV'. *SB*: Blue, two narrow white lines in entre, narrow red line near top and bottom edges, ound silver clasp with crown and star.

Royal Army Medical Corps

Facings: Dull cherry, *DC*: Blue, dull-cherry band nd piping. *SH*: Dull-cherry body and tip, dark- lue flaps and peak, gold piping to body and flaps, wo buttons. *Bt*: Blue, dull-cherry patch behind adge. *CB*: As cap badge, snakes facing inwards. *B*: Brass, with cap badge. *ST*: Soldiers only, brass, RAMC'. *L*: Dull cherry. First Aid Instructors wear brass arm badge as cap badge minus crown, with scroll bearing their title. *SB*: Three equal stripes, crimson over dark blue over yellow; brown buckles, left. WOIs' warrant badges outlined dull cherry.

Royal Army Ordnance Corps

Facings: Scarlet. *SH*: Blue body, flaps and peak, red piping to body, two buttons *Bt*: Blue. *CB*: As cap badge, muzzles inwards. *B*: As cap badge minus Garter and lower scroll. *L*: Red and blue, left shoulder. WOIs' warrant badges outlined red. *SB*: blue, three narrow red stripes; round silver buckle-plate with cap-badge minus lower scroll within peripheral inscription 'ROYAL ARMY ORDNANCE CORPS'. *C*: Blue.

Corps of Royal Electrical and Mechanical Engineers

Facings: Scarlet. *SH*: Scarlet body piped yellow, blue flaps piped gold, blue peak, two buttons. *Bt*: Blue. *CB*: As cap-badge minus top scroll, horses face inwards. *B*: Brass, as cap badge minus top scroll. WOIs' warrant badges outlined blue. *SB*: Blue, two stripes each red over yellow; round silver buckle-plate with cap-badge minus scrolls and motto 'ARTE ET MARTE'.

Corps of Royal Military Police

Facings: Scarlet. *DC*: Scarlet, blue band, scarlet piping. *SH*: Scarlet body and tip, blue flaps and peak. *Bt*: Scarlet. *CB*: As cap badge, silver for officers. *B*: Brass, with crowned, wreathed cypher as cap badge. Officers wear *L*: Red, left shoulder. *ST*: Brass, 'RMP'. *SB*: Red; brown buckles, left. WOIs' warrant badges outlined scarlet. On duty, personnel wear red brassard with black 'MP' on right arm, and silver whistle chain from top jacket buttonhole to left breast pocket; white belt, crossbelt, holster. *C*: Red.

Royal Pioneer Corps

Facings: Scarlet. *SH*: Blue body and peak, scarlet tip, blue flaps piped scarlet above green, two buttons. *Bt*: Blue. *CB*: As cap-badge, silver for officers. *B*: Brass, with cap-badge. *ST*: Soldiers only, brass, 'RPC'. WOIs' warrant badges outlined scarlet. *L*: Red and green, left shoulder. *SB*: Dark-blue with narrow centre stripes of red over green; round silver buckle with cap-badge.

Parachute Regiment WOI wearing officer-style bronze collar badges and Sam Browne belt. The maroon-and-light-blue lanyard identifies Parachute Brigade Headquarters. Note the Recruiter's arm badge; crossed Union Flags under a crown in heraldic colours on a scarlet backing. (*Soldier* **Magazine**)

Women's Royal Army Corps

Facings: Beech-brown. *DC:* Piper-green, black peak and strap. *Bt:* Piper-green, with raindrop-shaped beech-brown patch behind badge for Other Ranks. See colour plate D for cut of uniform. Only officers and WOIs wear golden rose *CB* with 'WRAC' in diamond formation. *B:* Brass, with coronet and cypher 'M' of Princess Royal, Controller Commandant of WRAC. Personnel serving with RMP wear special cap with scarlet crown and piper-green band, and red brassard. Rank badges, dark-green on beech-brown.

Intelligence Corps

Facings: Green. *DC:* Blue, cypress-green band and piping. *SH:* Cypress-green body piped grey, green flaps and tip, grey peak, two buttons. *Bt:* Cypress-green. *OSD:* Silver cap-badge. *CB:* As cap-badge, silver. *B:* Brass, crown over rose bloom. *L:* Cypress-green. *SSD:* As officers, but cap and *CB* brass. WOIs' warrant badges outlined green. *ST:* Brass 'INT CORPS' in arc.

Parachute Regiment soldiers in Bermuda. Clearly visible are the Denison smock, lightweight olive trousers, puttees, DMS boots (no special jump-boot is found necessary), maroon berets and '58-pattern webbing. On the right smock sleeves can be seen the trained parachutist's wings badge. (*Soldier Magazine*)

The Plates

(Notes have been kept to a minimum since all uniform information may be found in the body of the text.)

A1 General, Tropical Service Dress

No. 1 Dress hat and Sam Browne belt are formal dress; for everyday duty the khaki No. 2 Dress cap with red band and badge as illustrated, are worn. With combat dress this badge is worn on a blue beret. Many general officers retain their old regimental berets, however, worn with this badge e.g., khaki for Guards or Royal Anglians, dark green for Royal Green Jackets or Light Infantry, black for RTR, etc. 'EIIR' shoulder cypher indicates appointment as ADC to the Sovereign. This selection of decorations is typical of a general who has served from the Second World War to the present day.

A2 Major, Scots Guards, No. 2 Dress

The rather dark khaki and the short cap peak are typical of Foot Guards; the small patch of miniaturized Royal Stewart tartan above each

Lieutenant, Parachute Regiment and attached Staff Sergeant, REME, training with the Israeli UZI sub-machine gun. The officer wears the maroon stable belt, and the NCO that of REME. Both wear khaki combat shirts, the officer the lightweight trousers and the NCO the obsolete olive drab combat trousers. Both wear maroon berets and parachutist's 'wings'. (*Soldier* Magazine)

chinstrap button, and the buttons spaced in threes, are regimental features.

A3 Corporal, 10th Gurkha Rifles (Princess Mary's Own), Tropical Parade Dress

Heavily starched and creased Olive Drab uniform typical of British troops in the Far East, with regimental cap badge on typical Gurkha Kilmarnock. On the right shoulder would be worn the formation sign of the Singapore garrison, a black cat on yellow, and on the left the crossed white kukris on dark green of the Gurkha Infantry Brigade. The corporal is in the 'unfix bayonets' stance during guard mounting parade, in order to present his kukri for inspection. In traditional Rifles fashion, the rifle sling is worn slack.

B1 Colour Bearer, Royal Hampshire Regiment

Parade dress for most regiments consists of brightening up the No. 2 Dress with No. 1 Dress cap and various minor 'tribal items'. Note sword strap wound around hilt, as customary for dismounted officers. The bandolier and the Regimental Colour are in the regimental facing colour, the latter bearing some of the battle-honours awarded during the regiment's service; usually there are too many for more than a selection to be shown. Together with the Queen's Colour, this flag embodies the entire history of the regiment; they are always accorded full military honours.

B2 Sergeant, 5th Royal Inniskilling Dragoon Guards, No. 2 Dress

This regiment shares with the Royal Irish Rangers the distinction of green No. 2 Dress trousers. The white horse of Hanover on green worn as an arm badge by all this regiment's NCOs, recalls the origins of the British monarchy in the 18th century. The brassard indicates the Provost Sergeant in charge of Regimental Police.

B3 Corporal, Royal Hussars, No. 2 Dress

Crimson trousers and hat are inherited from the 11th Hussars, who also wore a red-brown beret with a 1-in. crimson headband without a badge. After amalgamation with the 10th Hussars the beret lost its headband but acquired the badge illustrated here on the No. 1 Dress hat, worn on a crimson oval-topped patch. This 'English'-pattern jacket is worn by all soldiers except those of the Scottish Division. As in other cavalry regiments, the NCO wears a regimental badge above his chevrons on the right arm; WOs wear the badge below their warrant badges. The absence of collar badges in No. 2 Dress is unusual among non-Guards regiments.

C1 Lance Corporal, Royal Military Police

The red and blue peaked cap may now be replaced by a scarlet beret. The red and black brassard is worn when on duty; the chevron on the lower left sleeve indicates two and a half years' impeccable service; and the crossed flags indicate a signaller. The new white plastic pistol belt for the Browning automatic has been introduced experimentally as a labour-saving feature.

Corporal of Royal Military Police in shirtsleeve order. Red and blue No. 1 Dress cap, obsolete khaki flannel shirt, No. 2 Dress trousers and DMS boots. Note red and black brassard, silver whistle chain, and white plastic equipment.

C2 Company Sergeant Major, Royal Scots

Trews are in Hunting Stewart, No. 8. The black cock's feathers are worn in the Glengarry for parades. The red sash is worn by CSMs of infantry and dismounted corps when performing the duty of Orderly Officers, and by sergeants and staff sergeants when acting as Orderly Sergeant. The '37-pattern belt is worn here. The badge worn below the rank crown on the left cuff indicates a qualified parachutist, but not a fully trained member of the airborne forces. The medals show that this NCO has seen service in Korea (the 'Butcher's Apron' ribbon), Kenya during the Mau Mau campaign, and—from the clasps on his General Service Medal—at least two other post-war trouble-spots. The bronze oakleaf indicates a mention in despatches for distinguished service.

C3 Staff Sergeant, King's Troop Royal Horse Artillery, Winter Stable Dress

This NCO serving (perhaps for as long as ten years) with this elite ceremonial and display unit wears a stiff-topped khaki SD cap reminiscent of the First World War, a heavy wool jersey, light khaki Bedford-cord breeches and black 'butcher' boots. Note white cannon between crown and chevrons. Patches: Royal Stewart (top left), Mackenzie (right) and Leslie tartans.

D1 Captain, Women's Royal Army Corps, Service Dress

Members of the WRAC are generally attached to corps where their clerical and technical skills are most useful—Royal Corps of Signals, RAOC, RCT, etc.—and some serve with the RMP. The corps is indicated by a single corps collar badge (here, Royal Signals) worn high on the left breast. Only officers wear the gold rose collar badges illustrated. In uniform, black court shoes are worn, matching the gloves and shoulder-bag, and a dark green 'tab' replaces the conventional tie. Note green shoulder-strap piping.

D2 Lieutenant, King's Regiment, Summer Barrack Dress

The unusual side hat, without buttons, peak or flaps as such, recalls that of the 4th/7th Royal Dragoon Guards. Officers of this regiment wear a light blue-grey shirt reminiscent of old Indian Army issue, a memento of Indian service. Officers in many regiments wear brass shoulder titles with

The last animal transport unit in the British Army was disbanded in Hong Kong in 1975. This shows a Royal Corps of Transport driver in No. 1 Dress cap, SD jacket and light Bedford cord breeches. The lanyard is white, and a white 5-point star—the driver's badge—would be worn on the upper right arm. The brown leather belt has an open-frame brass buckle. (MOD)

shirt-sleeve order and jerseys; soldiers frequently do not. The stable belt, worn by most units, is said to originate in the spare girth carried round the waist by cavalry troopers of a bygone age. This officer wears the new Barrack Dress trousers and traditional 'veldschoen'.

D3 Lieutenant, Queen Alexandra's Royal Army Nursing Corps, No. 2 Dress
Similar in design but differing in colour from the WRAC uniform, this costume has red-piped shoulder straps. Officers wear collar badges; NCOs

wear dark grey stripes on red backing. In temperate zone grey ward dress, officers wear the traditional red cape and red cuffs; in white tropical ward dress, red shoulder straps only.

E1 Lieutenant Pilot, Army Air Corps, Flying Clothing
Apart from liaison and casualty evacuation, AAC

WRAC Corporal of 176 Provost Coy., RMP, on security duty in Londonderry, 1972. Being attached to the RMP she wears the WRAC No. 1 Dress cap with a scarlet crown. Over her lovat-green No. 2 Dress she wears the Fragmentation Vest. (*Soldier Magazine*)

helicopters and light fixed-wing aircraft serve as military observation posts and in ground-support roles with anti-tank guided weapons. The flying clothing is conventional, but note ID disc clipped to breast. 'Flak jackets' are issued, but it is rumoured that in view of the danger of ground fire AAC crews prefer to sit on them!

E2 Radio Operator, Light Infantry, Temperate DPM Combat Dress
In practice the radio operator is normally a private, but we have shown here the dark-green on maize-yellow rank chevron worn in the Light Infantry. The Sterling SMG is carried, as the SLR is too bulky for a man burdened by a radio. The DPM combat cap is not worn much by infantry units, who generally prefer to retain 'tribal' headgear.

E3 Corporal, 2nd Royal Tank Regiment, Combat Dress
Although issued with DPM Combat Dress, the RTR prefer the black coverall originally issued for servicing duties; it is peculiar to the RTR, other armoured regiments wearing Olive Drab coveralls. Regimental identity is indicated by coloured shoulder strap slides and cravats; here the yellow, red, brown, green slide and yellow cravat identify

2nd RTR. The infantry are nowadays entirely equipped with '58-pattern webbing in temperate areas and '44-pattern in the tropics, but in other arms the old '37-pattern can still be found, as here—note the RTR regimental feature of black webbing.

F1 Gurkha Rifleman, Olive Drab Tropical Combat Dress
The scarlet hat-band identifies the 2nd Gurkha Rifles. The '44-pattern webbing is suitable for jungle service as it absorbs little moisture. The Armalite carbine, short and light, is suitable for the cramped environment and short combat ranges of such operations.

F2 Infantryman, Tropical DPM Combat Dress (No. 9 Dress)
This light uniform, in the same DPM pattern as for temperate zones but with a shirt-jacket which can be worn inside or over the trousers, is currently replacing the Olive Drab issue worn by figure F1. The bush-hat is of the same design as that of the previous uniform. This soldier carries the General Purpose Machine Gun (GPMG, 'Jimpy' to the troops), the belt-fed replacement of the famous Bren LMG; in its light role, as here, it has a folding bipod, but it can be tripod-mounted for sustained fire.

F3 Private, Royal Anglians, Arctic Combat Dress
Part of the British Army is equipped, trained and constantly ready to operate in support of the Norwegian Army on NATO's northern flank in the Arctic Circle. The white windproof smock and trousers and Canadian 'mukluks' are worn over DPM cold-weather dress with quilted thermal liner and cold-weather boots. The snow mittens have sheepskin pads on the back so that the wearer can remove the inevitable 'dew drop' from the nose without removing the glove and risking frostbite! The pack is the Bergen Rucksack. Goggles to prevent snow-blindness are issued, and weapons are camouflaged with white tape.

G1 Soldier in infantry role, Northern Ireland Riot Gear
The infantry are not the only corps to serve in this role; artillerymen, cavalrymen, engineers and other corps have all been exposed to this ordeal. The new 'Combat Helmet Northern Ireland'

illustrated was developed at great speed; the visor is acid-proof, and the wide chinstrap offers better protection from other hazards. Body armour is essential; the inevitable lack of mobility is a price worth paying when soldiers are required to stand steady under a hail of missiles from the mob.

Private, Royal Corps of Transport on security duty in Northern ireland. The strain placed on the Army's manpower by the requirements of this province has resulted in many units apart from combat infantry serving in the security forces in Ulster. The Fragmentation Vest is seen here in its old configuration; non-slip pads have now been fitted to the shoulders and the pockets have been moved down. The SLR is seen here with a night-sight. (*Soldier* Magazine)

G2 Ammunition Technician, RAOC, EOD Suit Mk 2
The Explosive Ordnance Disposal suit was rapidly developed due to the need to protect these highly trained specialists. The helmet has a heavy plastic visor and built-in radio communications.

G3 Private, Royal Regiment of Fusiliers, Northern Ireland
In summer the lightweight trousers illustrated are worn with shirt-sleeve order, in place of the heavier DPM suit. This concession to comfort is largely negated by the constant need to wear the fragmentation vest, recently improved by adding non-slip pads to the shoulders, to prevent the rifle-butt slipping off the smooth nylon. The respirator case is worn on the belt, and he carries the riot gun which fires 'baton rounds'. The distinctive fusilier headgear is rarely worn nowadays; most soldiers, especially patrols in rural areas, go bareheaded to avoid recognition by terrorist observation posts.

H1 Regimental Sergeant Major, The Gordon Highlanders, No. 2 Dress (Parade Order)
The Sam Browne belt is the symbol of appointment of this Warrant Officer 1st Class. The kilt is of 'Gordon' tartan—the military tartan devised for the Black Watch but with a yellow overstripe. White parade spats are worn here.

H2 Private, Parachute Regiment, Battle Jumping Order
He wears a post-war development of the cherished Denison Smock, with ribbed woollen cuffs and a camouflage pattern peculiar to airborne forces. The camouflage-net face veil is worn as a cravat. The parachutist's helmet illustrated is soon to be replaced by a glass-reinforced plastic model. The popular lightweight trousers are worn with short puttees. The main parachute is worn on the back, the reserve on the chest; below this is his fighting equipment in a container. His weapon is carried in a container in the crook of the right arm, and is lowered to hang on a strap during the jump.

H3 Possible Service Dress for the 1980s
For some time studies have been carried out on a parade uniform to replace No. 1 and No. 2 Dress, involving one basic design of hat, jacket and

Army guard dog with handler on security duty in Northern Ireland; note riot baton. (*Soldier* Magazine)

trousers onto which individual regiments can put their 'tribal items' such as facing colours, chevrons and badge backings, collar, cap and shoulder badges, hat bands, epaulettes, belts, buttons and gloves. This figure shows a *possible* future configuration for a sergeant of the Light Infantry. The unmatched jacket and trousers would ease provision of uniform and would achieve economies. The regimental facings are worn on the hat band and on detachable shoulder-boards, which latter bear black bugle-horns over 'LI'. How the Guards, the Irish and the Scottish regiments would be accommodated in this new system has yet to be decided. Surprisingly enough, surveys of soldiers' opinions on possible new uniforms have revealed little support for the re-introduction of the traditional red coat of the British soldier. Patches: l. to r., Douglas, Cameron of Erracht, and MacDuff tartans.

INDEX

Figures in **bold** refer to illustrations.